The Preached Word

READY OR NOT

Here I Come

Written By:

Gwendolyn R. Gathers

Order this book online at www.trafford.com
or email orders@trafford.com

Most Trafford titles are also available at major online book retailers.

Printed in the United States of America.

ISBN: 978-1-4269-9310-7 (sc)
ISBN: 978-1-4269-9311-4 (e)

Library of Congress Control Number: 2011915427

Trafford rev. 01/06/2012

 www.trafford.com

North America & international
toll-free: 1 888 232 4444 (USA & Canada)
phone: 250 383 6864 ♦ fax: 812 355 4082

READY OR NOT
HERE
I
COME!

Gwendolyn Rebecca Gathers
G. R. G. MINISTRIES

Reference used
The Holy Bible- King James Version
Old Testament / New Testament
The Living Bible
Webster's Dictionary

Acknowledgements

Robert Gathers, Jr.

Antwonn Gathers

Antonio Gathers

Adrian Gathers

Barbara Miles

Catherine Gathers

Gerald Mackey

Vermell Glover

Family and Friends

CONGRATULATIONS

Gad,

Congratulations on this new ministry.

"Therefore, my beloved, be steadfast, unmovable, always abounding in the work of the lord, for as mush as you know that your labor is not in vain in the lord".

(1st Corinthians 15:58)

You are truly an inspiration to me, for "a woman who fears the Lord is to be praised".

Our home is blessed with your loving touch. We appreciate you for always giving of yourself and sacrificing much for us.

How do I say thank you to someone who is a part of every dream I have?

God Bless!

YOU GO GIRL!
LOVE,

YOUR HUSBAND
BISHOP ROBERT GATHERS, JR.

TO MY SISTER

"Oh, magnify the Lord with me, let us exalt His name together" because the more we praise Him, the more He blesses us!

Congratulations on the success of your book! I always knew you could do it. Keep up the good work and continue to rely on your true strength, the Lord God Almighty!

Love always,
Your Lil Sis
Marline "Cynthia" Robinson

To Gwen,
The more you write, the more God will bless you. May your writing touch the hearts of those who read it. Sermons from God are messages to His people. May we take heed to what the Holy Spirit has to say.
Congratulations on your wonderful success.

Love always, your little adopted Sister
Qwanteria Pamela Marie Hall

A note from the Author

I would like to thank God for inspiring me to write this small, but powerful book, "The Preached Word". I hope it will encourage you in your daily walk with God. If you're not walking with God, I'm sure you will be thinking about it seriously before you're through reading this book.

To my family and friends - Thank you for your faith in me, your prayers, and your words of encouragement.

This book is humbly dedicated to everyone who reads it. It is written for the purpose of increasing your awareness to the fact that Christ is coming back for a church without spot or wrinkle, and to help you prepare yourself for His return.

It is written in the memory of our Lord and Savior Jesus Christ, who died that we might have a right to the tree of life.
Gwendolyn Rebecca Gathers

G. R. G. Ministries

To the readers,

Evangelist Gathers is a highly anointed woman of God. She is a wife, mother and a true inspiration to many. Through many trials, tribulations and victories, she continues to spread the love of Jesus Christ to all who comes in her path. I know you will be blessed with the words that God has laid on her heart to share.

Lovingly,
Arcina Suber

G. R. G. MINISTRIES

"The Preached Word"

Introduction

This book is a written version of my first sermon. It is not a story or an autobiography, so please do not read it as such. It is simply the preached word, written in a simple manner for easy reading.

As you read it, think of actually being in church, and hearing me preach. No, I did not preach this whole book, but I did preached on every subject matter that you will read later on in Galatians Chapter 5.

I was in my early thirties, sitting in church when God gave me this message. The preacher was preaching about being ready to go back with Jesus when He comes. That's when God spoke to me and said, "READY OR NOT, HERE I COME!"

"Write it down and study it, this is going to be the message for your initial sermon."

I preached that message on my forty-seventh birthday, Sunday, September 19, 1999.

During the years before my initial sermon, the Lord has given me several messages. I would study them and write them down. I did not know that God would have me put them in a book form, and that you would be reading one right now.

A few months after I preached that initial sermon, the Lord told me to write the books and title the series, "The Preached Word".

I trust you will be blessed by this word.

"The Preached Word"

SERMON 1
READY OR NOT, HERE I COME!

Revelations Chapter 22:1-7

Verse 1
"AND HE SHOWED ME A PURE RIVER OF WATER OF LIFE, CLEAR AS CRYSTAL, PROCEEDING OUT OF THE THRONE OF GOD AND OF THE LAMB.

Verse 2
IN THE MIST OF THE STREET OF IT, AND ON EITHER SIDE OF THE RIVER, WAS THERE THE TREE OF LIFE, WHICH BARE TWELVE MANNER OF FRUITS, AND YIELDED HER FRUIT EVERY MONTH; AND THE LEAVES OF THE TREE WERE FOR THE HEALING OF THE NATIONS.

Verse 3
AND THERE SHALL BE NO MORE CURSE: BUT THE THRONE OF GOD AND THE LAMB SHALL BE IN IT; AND HIS SERVANTS SHALL SERVE HIM;

Verse 4
AND THEY SHALL SEE HIS FACE; AND HIS NAME SHALL BE IN THEIR FOREHEADS.

Verse 5

AND THERE SHALL BE NO NIGHT THERE; AND THEY NEED NO CANDLE, NEITHER LIGHT OF THE SUN; FOR THE LORD GOD GIVETH THEM LIGHT; AND THEY SHALL REIGN FOREVER AND EVER

Verse 6

AND HE SAID UNTO ME, THESE SAYINGS ARE FAITHFUL AND TRUE: AND THE LORD GOD OF THE HOLY PROPHETS SENT HIS ANGEL TO SHOW UNTO HIS SERVANTS THE THINGS WHICH MUST SHORTLY BE DONE.

Verse 7

BEHOLD, I COME QUICKLY: BLESSED IS HE THAT KEEPETH THE SAYINGS OF THE PROPHECY OF THIS BOOK."

READY OR NOT, HERE I COME

John was describing some of the things he saw in the New Jerusalem. He was describing "The River Of Life", in The Holy City, where you and I hope to reside one day; a new place, in a new city, with a new address and zip code. We're not just going to have a new home. For the Lord said, "He has prepared for us a mansion." Not a cabin in the sky, or a room.
Can you imagine all of us fitting into a cabin or a room? *No!* Jesus is preparing us a mansion.

John 14:2 says, "IN MY FATHER'S HOUSE ARE MANY MANSIONS." That tells me that God's house is called Heaven, and in His house I have a mansion. It does not matter how many people get to heaven, everyone will have a mansion in that one heaven, where we will all dwell with the Father and with each other.

I don't care how much they sing the song, "Build Me A Cabin In Glory". Let me tell you that there are "NO CABINS" in Heaven. How is it going to look to have streets made of pure gold, twelve gates to the city, with each gate made of a single pearl, and when you walk through the gates you find nothing but log cabins?

I DON'T THINK SO!

God has a mansion for you, and if you live right, God's going to give it to you. I don't know how you feel, but I want what He promised and I won't settle for anything less! I don't want a cabin; and I'm not expecting one. That would be pretty tacky, don't you think? I certainly know that I'm not going through all of this suffering down here to receive a cabin. That's not what God promised His children. As a matter of fact, I don't believe the finest home here on earth can compare to the mansion God has prepared for you and me.

No more will we walk dusty, dirty, trashy, wet, muddy streets. We will finally be able to walk streets of gold. Jesus said, "I'm going away to prepare a place for you that where I am, there you may be also."

John said in Revelations Chapter 21, "THE STREETS WERE PURE GOLD," not pure as gold, but pure gold, "AND TRANSPARENT AS GLASS." You will be able to see your glorious reflection while walking the streets of gold.

The Bible says there will be a river of life in the New Jerusalem. And by the river of life will be twelve trees bearing twelve fruits, and the leaves on the trees will be for the healing of the nations.

No evil will be there - no murdering, no raping, no robbing, no fighting, and no cheating. NO SIN whatsoever will be in The

Holy City. It won't even get dark there. There will be no need for lamps or candles, flashlights or flares. No more cloudy days. No more dark nights because the sun will never go down. The Lord God will be our light, and we will reign with Him forever and ever.

When boaters go out to sea sailing, or on a fishing trip, they pack flares just in case they get in trouble. And if they get in trouble, they light the flares, and point them up towards the sky, so the rescuers can see the light, and rescue them.

Well, we won't need anyone to rescue us. We will be safe in the arms of Jesus. He will be our light in that city and we will reign with Him forever and ever. We will have His mark in our foreheads.

Revelations 22: 6-7 says, "The angel said unto me, these words are trust worthy and true. BEHOLD I COME QUICKLY."

God speaks to his prophets and reveals to them what will happen in the future. It is up to us to believe what they say, or not. The Bible says we are blessed if we believe what the prophets have said.

When Jesus appeared to the disciples for the second time, Thomas did not believe it was Jesus, until he saw the nail prints in Jesus' hand and saw the wound in his side. Thomas only believed because he saw. Jesus said, "BLESSED ARE THEY THAT HAVE NOT SEEN, AND YET BELIEVE." John 20:29

When I was a little girl, we played a game called "Hide And Seek". Several people could hide in this game at one time, but only one person could seek. The person that was chosen to seek was called "IT". Everyone else would hide. I didn't let anyone hide in the same place with me because they might stick out a little and we'd both be found. You had to find your own place to hide.

As everyone was running to find a hiding place, "IT" was counting to ten. One, two, three, four, five; and to make the game a little more fun, or to make you worry a little bit, "IT" would say five and a half, six, seven, eight, nine, ten. You had about ten seconds to find a place to hide. After "IT" reached the number ten, he or she would cry with a loud voice,

"READY OR NOT, HERE I COME"!

In the twelfth verse of Revelations Chapter 22, Jesus repeated Himself. He wanted you to know that these things are faithful and true. So as it was written, so let it be done.

"READY OR NOT, HERE I COME"!

Jesus is coming whether you're ready or not, and this is no game. He said "Behold I Come Quickly". You can run, but you can't hide. There will be no hiding place. Look for him! He's coming, and His reward is with Him to pay every man according to his work shall be. No ifs, ands or buts, no reckons, no maybe. He said it, it's true and He's coming. He's coming soon. When Jesus comes, we've got to be ready. We can't be getting ready. We must be already, ready.

God has given us a work to do and we cannot wait until its time for Him to come back to start. We must be about our Father's business right now, every day, while the blood is running warm in our veins.

You might get sick one day, lying on a bed of affliction, and you won't be able to do what God has told you to do. Then it will be to late. So while you still have health and strength, and you can get around, able to walk and talk, you need to be about your Father's business. But whether you do it or not, He's coming.

"READY OR NOT, HERE I COME!"

To be ready when Jesus comes, you must have your house in order. I'm not talking about the house you live in, the place where you go after a hard day at work. I'm talking about the house where your spirit lives - the house that is on the inside of you, which is your heart, soul and mind. The house where the Holy Ghost is supposed to reside. The house where the Holy

Ghost is supposed to live through you, but on the inside of you. Get that house in order.

We have got to get ready for the coming of the Lord. Too many people are concerned with dressing up the outside of their houses. They want to look pretty for the world. They want to show off their new clothes and their fine hats, their new shoes, their fine automobiles and their fine homes, when their souls are as black as night - dark and full of sin. Some people think that education and money will take them anywhere they want to go. That will work for you as long as you're here on earth, but if you want to go to heaven, and I believe you do, knowledge won't take you there and you can't buy your way. You must be born again of the water and of the spirit. [St. John 3:5] You must repent of your sins and live a holy life if you want to make heaven you eternal home.

We won't get to heaven with a sinful soul; we won't get to heaven with a sinful heart, and we won't get to heaven with a sinful mind. Our hearts soul and mind must be right with God - clean and pure. If we want to go back with Jesus when He comes, we've got to live right! Even if you don't live right, remember the message from God.

"READY OR NOT, HERE I COME

Galatians Chapter Five tells us of the things we need to get rid of before Jesus comes. Let me make them plain and easy to understand for you. A lot of times people want the preacher to excite them, and when their excited they forget more than half of what the preacher has said.

I must break the scriptures down so you may understand.

There's an old familiar saying, "If the shoe fits, wear it." I say to you, don't wear it. Kick them off your feet. Ask the Lord to give you a new pair. You don't have to wear those shoes of sin any longer.

Again I say, kick them off and ask God for a new pair - a new way of walking, a new way of talking, and a new way of thinking. Be ye transformed by the renewing of your mind. Don't be guilty of the same sins any longer!

The Word of God declares, "For if we confess our sins, He is faithful and just to forgive us, and cleanse us from all unrighteousness". 1st John 1:9

Here is what the bible says we must put out of our lives if we want to go to heaven when Jesus returns. And keep in mind these are just a few things, for all unrighteousness is sin.
All souls are mine says the Lord, but the soul that sinneth, it shall die. Ezekiel 18:4

GALATIANS 5:19-21
NOW THE WORKS OF THE FLESH ARE MADE MANIFEST,
WHICH ARE THESE:

1.   We must Put Away Adultery:
This is willful sexual intercourse with someone else's husband
or wife.

I wondered why Paul put this first. I believe it was because
flesh, back then, was the biggest problem to men and women,
and God knew it was going to be the biggest problem in men
and women lives today. Your worst enemy is your flesh. Your
flesh will cause you to do some serious harm to yourself and
to others. Flesh (your desires; the things that please you the
most; selfishness) will even cause you to lose your soul. Put
away adultery. Stop having sexual intercourse with someone
else's husband or wife. Now that's plain, simple, and to the
point.

Jesus said, "Whoever looks on a women to lust for her has
already committed adultery in his heart." But we see again
in the scriptures when the woman was caught in the act of
adultery and the people wanted to stone her to death, that same
Jesus came to her rescue and told her to "go and sin no more".
He is telling you today, "sin no more" (John 8:1-11). Our body
is the temple of the Holy Ghost.

2.   We must put away fornication:

This is single people engaging in sexual intercourse.

Paul states this second to include everybody. He says in Romans 13:13, "PUT YE ON THE LORD JESUS CHRIST, AND MAKE NO PROVISION FOR THE FLESH, TO FULFILL THE LUSTS THEREOF." We should spend our time getting to know the Lord Jesus, His will and His way for our lives. I know it's very hard for young people, and some not so young, to abstain from having sex before marriage; I was once young, so I know. It's even harder now when so much of it is on the television, in movies, and in commercials, for all to see day in and day out. You need the Holy Ghost to help you. If you desire a husband or a wife, God will give you one in His own time if you trust Him and wait for Him to do so. While you're waiting, just do as Jesus asks in Matthew 6:33

"SEEK YE FIRST THE KINGDOM OF GOD AND HIS RIGHTEOUSNESS, AND ALL THESE THINGS SHALL BE ADDED UNTO YOU".

Get to know God and what he wants for you. He will give you the desires of your heart.

3.   We must put away un-cleanness:

Wicked or evil sexual conduct or habit; Sexual immorality, such as prostitution, lesbianism, homosexuality, having sex with animals, child molestation, having sex with family members other than your spouse (incest).

You've got to put it away. This word is for saints and sinners. Just because you are a member of a church, does not mean you are not guilty of these works of the flesh. The bible says, "FOR THE TIME IS COME THAT JUDGMENT MUST BEGIN AT THE HOUSE OF GOD: AND IF IT FIRST BEGIN AT US, WHAT SHALL THE END BE OF THEM THAT KNOW NOT THE GOSPEL OF GOD?" 1st Peter 4:17

Now that tells me there are some people who go to church, that are guilty of the works of the flesh. So don't think you can join a church to hide the fact that you're living in sin, because it won't work. God's eye is on the little sparrow and I know He watches you and me. So put it away.

4.	We must put away lasciviousness:
Sexual desires that are immoral (as stated above), to include lewd acts that are aroused by fleshly lusts, lesbianism, homosexuality, having sex with animals.

Homosexuality is prohibited in the scriptures. Leviticus 18:22-30 reads,
"Thou shalt not lie with mankind, as with womankind: it is abomination.
Neither shalt thou lie with any beast to defile thyself therewith: neither shall any woman stand before a beast to lie down thereto: it is confusion.

Defile not ye yourselves in any of these things: for in all these the nations are defiled which I cast out before you:
And the land is defiled: therefore I do visit the iniquity thereof upon it, and the land itself vomiteth out her inhabitants.
Ye shall therefore keep my statutes and my judgments, and shall not commit any of these abominations; neither any of your own nation, nor any stranger that sojourneth among you:
(For all these abominations have the men of the land done, which were before you, and the land is defiled)
That the land spew not you out also, when ye defile it, as it spued out the nations that were before you.
For whosoever shall commit any of these abominations, even the souls that commit them shall be cut off from among their people.

Therefore shall ye keep mine ordinance, that ye commit not any one of these abominable customs, which were committed before you, and that ye defile not yourselves therein: I am the LORD your God."

Romans 1:21-32 "Because that, when they knew God, they glorified him not as God, neither were thankful; but became vain in their imaginations, and their foolish heart was darkened.

Professing themselves to be wise, they became fools, and changed the glory of the uncorruptible God into an image made like to corruptible man, and to <u>birds</u>, and fourfooted beasts, and creeping things.

Wherefore God also gave them up to uncleanness through the lusts of their own hearts, to dishonour their own bodies between themselves:
Who changed the truth of God into a lie, and worshipped and served the <u>creature</u> more than the Creator, who is blessed forever. Amen.

For this cause God gave them up unto vile <u>affections</u>: for even their women did change the natural use into that which is against nature:
And likewise also the men, leaving the natural use of the woman, burned in their *<u>lust</u>* one toward another; men with men working that which is unseemly, and receiving in themselves that recompence of their error which was meet,
and even as they did not like to retain God in their knowledge, God gave them over to a reprobate mind, to do those things which are not convenient;
Being filled with all unrighteousness, <u>fornication</u>, wickedness, <u>covetousness</u>, maliciousness; full of envy, murder, debate, deceit, malignity, whisperers,
<u>Backbiters</u>, haters of God, despiteful, proud, boasters, inventors of evil things, disobedient to parents, without understanding, covenantbreakers, without natural <u>affection</u>, implacable, unmerciful:

Who knowing the judgment of God, that they which commit such things are worthy of death, not only do the same, but have pleasure in them that do them.

Leviticus 20:13 says, "IF A MAN LIE WITH MANKIND, AS HE LIETH WITH A WOMAN, BOTH OF THEM HAVE COMMITTED AN ABOMINATION; THEY SHALL SURELY BE PUT TO DEATH; THEIR BLOOD SHALL BE UPON THEM".

In the 19th Chapter of Genesis, God destroyed the city of Sodom and Gomorrah for their uncleanness and lasciviousness. In the New Testament scriptures, (1 Corinthians 6:9), Paul teaches this;
"KNOW YE NOT THAT THE UNRIGHTEOUS SHALL NOT INHERERIT THE KINGDOM OF GOD? BE NOT DECEIVED: NEITHER FORNICATORS, NOR IDOLATERS, NOR ADULTERERS NOR EFFEMINATE, NOR ABUSERS OF THEMSELVES WITH MANKIND."

In this passage of scriptures, when Paul referred to mankind, he was referring to the human race. Lesbians are included in the judgments of God.
"All souls are mine saith the Lord, but the soul that sinneth, it shall die." You must repent of all your sins if you want to go back with Jesus when He comes.

5.　　We must put away Idolatry:
This is worshiping idol gods; worshiping something that is created rather than God the creator.

"THOU SHALT HAVE NO OTHER GOD BEFORE ME," is the first commandment. Anything you put before God, to praise and cherish, is an idol. It does not have to be a golden image. It could be your car, job, children, money, pleasure or friends. Anything you put before God or in front of God, to worship or cherish, instead of worshiping God, are idols. These things should never come before the will of God in your life. Remember, they can be taken away.

6.　　We must put away witchcraft:
This is practicing spells, soothsaying, palm reading and calling that 800 number on the telephone. You have to put it away!

I don't need anyone to tell me who my enemies are. I don't need anyone to tell me who to keep away from. I don't have to ask anyone how to restore my lost nature. They don't have to tell me my future because I already know. Jesus has already told me. If I want to know anything about my own self, all I have to do is pick up my Bible and read it. God's Word will tell me everything I want to know about myself - and about you too!

Why take your hard earned money, and give it to someone to tell you what you need to know about why you are going through certain things in your life? Pick up *your* Bible and read it for yourself. All answers to life situations are in the word of God. Put away witchcraft. Even if you don't, "READY OR NOT, HERE I COME!"

7.   We must put away hatred:
This means to feel animosity or hostility towards someone, with or without a cause.

I've heard my overseer, Apostle C. A. Keith, say several times "people will hate you for no reason at all." I did not understand what that meant for a long time. But I've learned the true meaning of that saying. People will hate you just because of who you are and what you are. You haven't done anything to them personally to cause them to hate you, they just don't like how you dress, what you stand for, your position in the church, the kind of car you drive, or just because your beliefs are different from theirs. As you live and breath, there is someone who hates you, even if it is just the devil.

People go around saying, "I don't like this one and I don't like that one"; and the most famous saying, "my spirit doesn't agree with him or her". If your sister or brother is operating in the wrong spirit, instead of talking about them and hating them, you need to help them - pray for them; witness to them and council with them, so they can get the right spirit within them. You can't go to Heaven by yourself and you can't get to

Heaven if you hate your brothers and sisters, and not just your brothers and sisters in Christ, you can't get to heaven if you hate anyone.

They haven't done anything to you, but because they are who they are, you hate them. You might say, "I love them; I just hate the lifestyle they live." Well if that's true, when was the last time you tried to get them to change their lifestyle? When was the last time you hugged your best friend whom you found out has A.I.D.S? What about the person who stole something from you? What about that son or daughter whose strung out on drugs, or the one who's a homosexual or lesbian? Think about it. Do you love them, or do you hate them? If you truly love them, you will be able to show them love in actions and not just in words. Love *is* an action word. 1st JOHN 4:15 says, "WHOSOEVER HATETH HIS BROTHER IS A MURDERER: AND YE KNOW THAT NO MURDERER HATH ETERNAL LIFE ABIDING IN HIM". We have to put away hatred.

8.   We must put away variance:
This means to change from day to day, supposing to be one way, but not; to be unstable.

Today you're on fire for the Lord, but the next day you're sitting in a bucket of ice. Today you're happy, and tomorrow you're mad with the whole world. Today you feel like talking and tomorrow you don't want to be bothered. You're up today, down tomorrow, unstable in your thoughts. God can't use you when you are unstable. We need to "be steadfast, unmovable, always abounding in the work of the Lord, for as much as you know your labor is not in vain in the Lord". [1st Corinthians 15:58] God can't use you if you're easy to be persuaded by everything that comes along in life. Settle yourself down, get rooted and grounded in Christ Jesus so He can use you in these last days.

Variance, supposing to be one way, but your not. When you're in church you're this person, but when you get on your job you're another person. When you go to the grocery store, you're someone else, when you get around your family and friends, your name changes. God wants you to be stable and sober minded. But whether you're stable or not, He's still coming.

9.   We must put away emulations:
This is selfish ambition: Having a constant effort to get the best for yourself, or to be better than someone else, even by crushing others character.

There is certainly nothing wrong with wanting to do your best, but you don't have to destroy someone else to achieve that. There is no need to crush someone's character or degrade them to make yourself look good.

Why do some people always try to out do or be "better than" the next person? Do we really need the attitude that "I could have done it better?" You make a constant effort to be the best, even if it means stepping on others. You have the attitude that you're going to be the best, no matter what you have to do or who you have to do it too. You've got to be number one. You will even turn on your best friend to be number one.

Sister Jones put on a program last month and everything turned out very well, but you still had the bad attitude that, "I could have done it better." So what! It was not your turn to do it.

Why do people feel they have to always be number one? Why can't you be number two sometimes? There is nothing wrong with being number two. Number two is just as important as number one. If number one didn't have number two, number one would not exist. Number one would not be where it is if it were not for number two.

If God called #one to preach and #two to carry the briefcase, and you're the one who carries the briefcase, do it to the glory of God and don't be upset. Number one is tired after preaching so hard and needs you to carry that briefcase!

10.   We must put away wrath: Anger, fits of rage, complaints, and criticisms and cursing.

These things you must put away before Jesus comes. These things generate from within and because you have to be holy from the inside out, you have to put it away.

You won't get to heaven with these works of the flesh present in your life. Anger and fits of rage will cause you to do something you will regret for the rest of your life. If you don't believe that, take a trip to the jailhouse, and see how many people are glad to be there. You will find many people there saying, "I didn't mean to do it". One wrong move or one wrong word could destroy your life. It is not a good thing to act before you think about what your about to do. Even when your complaining and criticizing, you could say something that will destroy someone else's life, when you didn't really mean to. Before you react, backtrack. Stop! Listen! Think about it!

11.   We must put away strife: Internal dissension; conflict within an organization or nation.

Paul said to Timothy, "I will therefore that men pray everywhere, lifting up holy hands, without wrath and doubting". 1st Timothy 2:8

When we go to God in prayer, our hearts and minds have to be pure. Should God overlook the fact that you have anger in your heart and answer your prayers anyway? Should He overlook the fact that you aren't speaking to your neighbor and continue to bless you without letting you know that your wrong?   I don't think so.

Jesus tells us in Matthew 5:22-24, that if we know our brother has an ought against us, we should not even give an offering until we have straightened the matter out. Why should God give us gifts with love and mercy in His heart, when we give Him gifts with anger, hatred and jealousy in ours?
Ephesians 5:26 says "BE YE ANGRY AND SIN NOT: LET NOT THE SUN GO DOWN ON YOUR WRATH". Straighten things out while you are with them. If you don't you might not get another chance. If you don't get it right, you won't be ready and God just might come.

We do not always think the same thoughts all the time. It's at those times when we disagree, that we need to be careful not to start conflicts in the body of Christ. You have heard it said so many times "we can disagree without being disagreeable". We should be able to express ourselves in an orderly manner. So many churches have split because of internal dissension. My husband preached a message once titled "It's An Inside Job", and it is. Strife generates from the inside of a person, and it can tear up a church, a home, an organization, and even a nation. Don't do it! Repent! Put it away!

12.   We must put away seditions: Open rebellion

The bible says we ought to obey them that have rule over us, but there are those who will not obey. To obey simply means to respect. If you have respect for them that have rule over you, you will obey them in righteous, with no problems. Some people have a hard time submitting to leaders. They want a preacher, but not a pastor. Just preach to me, but don't counsel me when I'm wrong. They are hardheaded and stiff necked. Everyone is wrong except them. They will verbally attack leadership and try to get others to agree with them. They are what I call fault-finders. Don't you know the more you look to see something wrong the more the devil will show you? He will take the smallest thing and cause you to turn it in to something that will stir up more trouble than it's worth. Stop finding fault with your leaders. Love them, pray for them, and respect them.

13   We must put away heresies: A difference of opinions in religious beliefs that causes division within the church.

This is what happens when there is open rebellion in the church. We have "groupies" in the church, a group over here and a group over there. One group is going to support this preacher and the other group will support that preacher. This should not be so, especially if you're planning to go to Heaven. You have to get rid of that attitude. God is not pleased with that, and He won't allow it in Heaven. So if you have it in you when He comes, certainly you won't be going back with Him.

You may still be in the same building, but you have caused so much confusion that the church breaks off into groups. We call it 'clicks". This person in this click don't like someone in that click. This group don't like that group. You sit over there and I'll sit over here. The choir is not speaking to the ushers and the ushers not speaking to the mothers and the list goes on and on. Is God please? NOWAY! How can we say we're going to heaven and we can't get along right down here. When we get to heaven there's going to be billions of people there. If we can't get along with 20 or 30, how are we going to handle billions. There's not going to be a section for your click up in heaven. Put away heresies. Our opinion doesn't matter anyway. It's God's way or no way at all.

Romans 10:3 "FOR THEY BEING IGNORANT OF GOD'S RIGHTEOUSNESS, AND GOING ABOUT TO ESTABLISH THEIR OWN RIGHTEOUSNESS, HAVE NOT SUBMITTED THEMSELVES UNTO THE RIGHTEOUSNESS OF GOD."

Our ways are not God's ways, neither are our thoughts His thoughts.

14.   We must put away envying: Jealousy; Being resentful of other people because they have something that you desire.

The 10th commandment says, "THOU SHALT NOT COVET THY NEIGHBOR'S HOUSE, THOU SHALT NOT COVET THY

NEIGHBOR'S WIFE, NOR HIS MANSERVANT, NOR HIS MAIDSERVANT, NOR HIS OX, NOR HIS ASS, NOR ANYTHING THAT IS THY NEIGHBOR'S." Exodus 20:17

FOOD FOR THOUGHT:
Again I say, the only reason you're jealous of someone else is because you're unhappy with your own life. If you were satisfied with what God is doing in your life, you would be zealous and not jealous.

And that's all I have to say about that.

15.   We must put away murdering: Killing a person unlawfully and with malice.

There are many reasons why people kill. Most killings are done unlawfully and with malice. Murders that are not intentional are called "accidental death". Even if you kill someone accidentally, you still need God's forgiveness, for the sixth commandment says "Thou shalt not kill". And what about the murdering that we commit with that unruly member of our body called the tongue. The things we say about people, even the things we say to people, can kill their self-esteem and make them feel that they have no self worth. You can kill a person just by what you say to them. A saint who is not so strong will leave the church, and backslide because of what someone says. You could cause a sinner to never come to Christ, if you say the wrong thing. It's not so much what we say but, rather, the tone of voice we say it in. Be careful how you talk to people. There's a time to cry loud and spare not, and there's a time to remember the Scripture that declares, "With loving kindness have I drawn thee."

16.   We must put away drunkenness: being controlled by alcoholic drinks.

1ˢᵗ Peter 4:7 says, "BUT THE END OF ALL THINGS ARE AT HAND; THEREFORE BE SOBER, AND WATCH UNTO PRAYER". The end of this world is coming. Jesus will be back to gather His own, and a drunk man will not be ready to go back with Him when He comes. The drunken man will be mentally and physically impaired. We have to be alert to the signs of the time we are living in.

17.   We must put away reveling: To engage in uproarious festivities.

This means having or going to wild parties and all other things of the same sort. Some people that go to church are still going to the nightclubs. Some people that sing the gospel of Jesus Christ still sing the devil's songs. Paul said "I have told you once and I'm telling you again, anyone who is guilty of these things will not inherit the kingdom of God.

If you're guilty of any of these things, you are not ready for the coming of the Lord. If any of these things are present in your spirit you will not go to heaven.

Most churches will tell you when you join, "Give me your hand and give God your heart," but I say to you, you need to give God more than your heart. You need to give Him your life - your whole life – mind, body and soul. And those people that tell you it don't take all of that giving up things to get to heaven, it don't take all of that holy living to get to heaven, they lied to you. For Jesus said, "Except a man be born of the water and of the spirit, he can't even see the kingdom of God". You must be born again! St. John 3:5-7

It's going to take being born again and a whole lot more in order for you to go to heaven. Salvation is free, but to keep it yu have to pay a price called sacrifice.

"READY OR NOT, HERE I COME!"

(As it was revealed to me) "He's coming on a cloud and every eye shall see Him", but every eye will not go back with Him. Yes, they will see Him coming but they will not go back with Him. There will be some that think they're going back, but because they continue to commit adultery, fornication, uncleanness, lasciviousness, idolatry, witchcraft, hatred, variance, emulations, wrath, strife, seditions, heresies, envying, murders, drunkenness, reveling and have not repented, their eyes will see Him, but they won't go back with Him. Nevertheless, READY OR NOT, HERE I COME.

Romans 6:1-4 says, "WHAT SHALL WE SAY THEN? SHALL WE CONTINUE IN SIN THAT GRACE MAY ABOUND? GOD FORBID. HOW SHALL WE WHO ARE DEAD TO SIN, LIVE ANY LONGER THERE IN? KNOW YE NOT, THAT SO MANY OF US AS WERE BAPTIZED INTO JESUS CHRIST WERE BAPTIZED INTO HIS DEATH? THEREFORE WE ARE BURIED WITH HIM BY BAPTISM INTO DEATH: THAT LIKE AS CHRIST WAS RAISED UP FROM THE DEAD BY THE GLORY OF THE FATHER, EVEN SO WE ALSO SHOULD WALK IN THE NEWNESS OF LIFE".

If you are walking in the newness of life, there would be no room in your life for the works of the flesh. For now you are in Christ Jesus, you are a new creature, old things are passed away, and behold all things are become new. [1st CORINTHIANS 5:17]

If you are guilty of any of the works of the flesh and Jesus Christ comes back, you won't go to heaven.

Who's going back with the Lord?
King David asked the question, "Lord, who shall abide in thy tabernacle, who shall dwell in thy holy hill?" Then he answered the question.

"HE THAT WALKETH UPRIGHTLY, AND WORKETH RIGHTEOUSNESS, AND SPEAKETH THE TRUTH IN HIS HEART". That's who's going back with Him.

No liar, no thief, no whoremonger, and no backbiter will be there! If you have any ill feelings about anybody, I admonish you to get rid of it today. Get those things out of your heart, and be ye ready when Jesus comes.

Who else is going to heaven?

He that presents his body a living sacrifice, holy, acceptable unto God, which is your reasonable service. If you want to go back with the Lord, you must present your whole body to Him. That's why I said you just couldn't give God your heart and that's all. You have to give Him everything you've got. Give Him your heart, hands, feet, eyes, mouth, legs - your whole body – a holy body from head to toe. Not only does your body have to be holy, but it also has to be acceptable unto God. And this is just your reasonable service. You owe God that. Some of you, He has already saved, sanctified you, filled you with the Holy Ghost, blessed you, kept you, made ways out of nowhere for you, and opened doors for you that no man could close, so it's just your reasonable service.

Who else is going back with the Lord?

"He that backbiteth not with his tongue, nor doeth evil to his neighbor, nor taketh up a reproach to his neighbor". He that hath clean hands and a pure heart, who hath not lifted his soul unto vanity, nor sworn deceitfully. Nevertheless,

"READY OR NOT, HERE I COME!"

John said, "I heard the number of them, which were sealed: and there were sealed a hundred and forty and four thousand, of all the tribes of the children of Israel". After this I beheld, and, lo, a great multitude, which no man could number, of all races, all nations, all different languages, black men, white men, China men, rich men, poor men, standing before the throne of God saying worthy is the lamb that was slain to receive power.

If you want to be in that number, you must be blood washed and born again! Born of the water and of the spirit. You must be redeemed.

There is a song in my heart that the angels can't sing "Redeemed, Redeemed, I've Been Washed In The Blood Of The Lamb! God has written my name in the Lamb's book of life - I've been redeemed!

You see the angels did not sin, so they did not need a Savior; the angels have never been sick, so they don't know Jesus as a healer. The angels never had a door closed in their face, so they don't know that Jesus could open doors that no man could close. The angels don't have bills that need to be paid, so they have not experienced the fact that my father is rich in houses and land, or that He holds the world in the palm of his hands. He promised to supply all our needs according to His riches in glory by Christ Jesus. Oh, I have a song that the angels cannot sing, "Redeemed, Redeemed, I've been washed in the blood of the Lamb! [*Hallelujah*]

"READY OR NOT HERE I COME!"

Revelations 22:11 "He that is unjust, let him be unjust still, he which is filthy let him be filthy still, and he that is righteous let him be righteous still, and he that is holy let him be holy still". Whatever state the Lord finds you in, you're going to be just that.

The very second that Jesus comes, the very moment that he cracks the sky, whatever state He finds you in, you're going to stay in that state, and it's going to be to late for you to do anything about it. If he finds you lying, you will keep right on lying. If he finds you in adultery, you will stay right there. If He finds you out of the ark of safety, you will stay right there. Jesus says, "ready or not, here I come", and I'm coming quickly and my reward is with me, to pay every man, according to his work shall be.

What kind of work are you doing and what are you working for? Are you working the works of the flesh that will guarantee you a place in hell with the devil and his angles, or are you working the works of the sprit that will guarantee you eternal life with Christ?

Galatians 5:22-23

"But the fruit of the spirit is love, joy, peace, longsuffering, gentleness, goodness, faith, meekness, temperance, against such there is no law.

Christ said I'm coming for a church without spot or wrinkle, without blemish, without sin, without malice, without hatred, without strife, and you must be ready to go back with Him when He comes. Nevertheless,

"READY OR NOT, HERE I COME!"

If you're not ready to go back with the Lord when He comes, right now, as you're reading this little book, you still have a chance to get ready. The blood is yet running warm in your veins, and whatever sin is in your life, Jesus can get you out of it. It does not matter what kind of sin you're in. No matter how long you've been in it, Jesus can get you out, and pick you up, if He has to reach way down-down-down.

His ear is not too heavy that He can't hear you, and His arm is not too short that He can't reach down and pull you out. Though your sins be as scarlet, He can make them white as snow. Though they be as red as crimson, He can make them as lambs wool. Jesus will forgive you and throw your sins into the sea of forgetfulness. Jesus can get you ready for His coming.

I want to be ready when He comes. I'm living to be ready when He comes. What about you?

We have heard for years that we're living in the last days, and because it's been said such a long time ago, and still being said, people think they have plenty of time. Some would even dare to say, "I can get saved on my sick bed and still go to heaven". This is true, but why take that chance? What if you have a massive heart attack and die in your sins? What if you have a fatal car accident or someone accidentally shoots you? Please don't take that chance.

Even if you're not ready, He's still coming. One reason why He has delayed His coming is to extend grace and mercy to you, and give you a chance to get ready.

1st JOHN: 1-9 SAYS "IF WE CONFESS OUR SINS, HE IS FAITHFUL AND JUST TO FORGIVE US OUR SINS, AND TO CLEANSE US FROM ALL UNRIGHTEOUSNESS".

2nd PETER 3:9 SAYS "THE LORD IS NOT SLACK CONCERNING HIS PROMISE AS SOME MEN COUNT SLACKNESS; BUT IS LONG-SUFFERING TO US-WARD, NOT WILLING THAT ANY PERISH, BUT THAT ALL SHOULD COME TO REPENTANCE".

It's not God's will that you die in sin to reap eternal damnation. He wants to forgive your sins and write your name in the Lambs book of life.

He said He was going away to prepare a place for us, that where He is, we could be there also. He is going to keep His promise, so "READY OR NOT, HERE I COME! "Don't let Him catch you with your work un-done.

Please don't take this message lightly. Jesus is coming back!

Have you ever told someone, [or has someone ever told you,] "I'll pick you up for church, be ready when I get there"? Well, when you get there, they're still not ready. They can't find the other shoe. The phone is ringing and they have to answer it. The house keys are missing and they can't find it. Maybe they over slept, and it's going to take them a while to get ready. So you decide to come back for them later. Or maybe their ready but just have that one little last minute thing to do, like comb their hair, slip on their shoes, or put on their jacket, and they yell to you "wait a minute, I'm coming! And you wait?

Not so when Jesus comes. If you are not ready, you will be left behind.

AND BEHOLD I COME QUICKLY; AND MY REWARD IS WITH ME, TO PAY EVERY MAN ACCORDING TO HIS WORK SHALL BE.

REV.22: 12

READY OR NOT, HERE I COME

Additional Scriptures

MATTHEW 1:21
JOHN 3:16-17
JOHN 10:1-18
1st PETER 2:1-3
JEREMIAH 31:3

ROMANS 6- 12:1-2
EPHASIANS 5
EXODUS 20:1-17

Have you accepted Jesus Christ as your personal Savior? If not, allow me to tell you of God's simple plan of salvation.

Romans 10:9-10 declares the following:

"If thou shalt confess with thy mouth the Lord Jesus, and shalt believe in thine heart that God hath raised Him from the dead, thou shalt be saved. For with the heart man believeth unto righteousness; and with the mouth confession is made unto salvation".

A PRAYER OF REPENTANCE

Father,
I come to you as humbly as I know how,
asking you to forgive me of all the sins
I have committed in thoughts words and deeds. Please come into my life, and
save me from eternal damnation.
I believe in Jesus Christ
as the scriptures proclaim.
I want to live for you the rest of my life.
Teach me, oh Lord, the way of thy statutes,
and I shall keep them unto the end of my life.
Give me understanding and I will keep your laws; I will observe them with my whole heart. In Jesus' name I pray, Amen
If you prayed that prayer and you really meant it with all your heart, the angels in heaven are rejoicing over your one little soul.
Praise God!!

READY OR NOT, HERE I COME

"Night Thief"

Ready or not, here I come,
to return for my people as
we all mount up as one.

It shall be done that all will call my name.
Believe that I am the Son of God
and be saved from hell's flame.

Don't be afraid like Peter. Stand up and fight.
Hold your head up and stick your chest out
For on your soul I'll shine a light.

Be prepared when I come back,
So you can be by my side, and
receive your wings like an eagle;
for you to soar, for you to glide.

 For you know not the time or the place,
but you know the event,
So I say today, you have time to repent.

For I shall return, whether you're ready or not;

Antwonn Gathers

Printed in the United States
By Bookmasters